FROM THE #248,948 TOP-SELLING AUTHOR OF *FAILURE STARTS WITH YOU* COMES:

YOU ONLY NEED THESE WORDS

A SIMPLIFIED APPROACH TO SELF-MOTIVATION

BY: P.J. STAZ

Table of Contents

Introduction

When discussing motivation, words matter. Specifically, the number of words used to get a message across. There are endless quotes to reflect on and books to read, but how many of those quotes do you truly need in order to embark on the path towards your best self? Most have the potential to be helpful, but the true measure is the ability for those words to get you to stop reading and start taking action.

This book strongly encourages you to not spend too much time reading, by providing a single, powerful quote that can motivate you at each critical moment when you have to choose between either taking a step towards your best self, or keep living as you are (i.e. your unfulfilled self). If you do choose to go past Chapter 1, it will be worth your effort and time as we will analyze further why these words are all you need.

The remaining content will guide you as quickly as possible, so that you can start incorporating the guiding quote into your life. The structure is designed to make you aware of the valuable time you have, so you can stop reading and simply get to it.

The content will specifically help you during the moments when you are faced with doing what you are meant to do, or choosing to delay action again.

The goal is to demonstrate this with succinct and less language than other motivational works. That is the purpose of this book – to inspire you and remind you how little you actually need to know before you can work towards that best self you know is in you.

And of course, there are other quotes that can motivate you, but this one is special as it targets that exact moment when you must choose to do or not do. The words in our message are all you really need to know and consider at those critical moments.

That is to say, right now.

Chapter 1:
The Only Page You Need to Read

This page contains the only quote you need to embark on the fastest path towards your best self.

Here it is:

**Focus, Work Smart, Execute Now,
and Everything Else Will Follow.**

Think about that for a moment. Does it make sense?

If so, then use this every day starting now.

Easy enough, right?

Then that's it.

You only need these words.

Chapter 2:
Don't Read Any Further

Guess not?

The quote was too simple to connect with it so quickly.

More words are required then.

Chapter 3:
It Really Is That Easy

It really is that easy.

Reread the first chapter, then stop reading.

That was really the only page you needed to read (and you know it!).

Oh, you came back?

The quote is easy to understand for everyone. All you have to do is apply it to your life.

However, for some reason, we do not feel ready. We do not feel ready to succeed <u>right now</u>.

This is normal. Too often, we feel we need more before we can begin on the journey towards our best self.

Specifically, we feel we need more words and preparation to allow us to begin.

We think other things need to happen or align before we are able to start on that path.

We tell ourselves that now is not the right time, and we always promise ourselves that we will do it soon.

We choose not to be ready.

The quote remedies this quickly, if implemented with dedication.

So how do we get you to stop reading and start working right now to implement those simple words?

How quickly can we do this?

Perhaps putting the words into a nice script will be more motivational?

Focus, Work Smart, Execute Now,
and Everything Else Will Follow.

Is that better?

Great.

Now simply go and do that.

After a few seconds of reflection, again you will see that this is all you really need from this book.

Nope, that didn't work.

Okay, maybe there is more to learn?

But seriously, after these next pages, you are good to go even if you don't realize it.

The key is to just start. Start before you think you are ready.

You know that though. You think of that often, so to reinforce the message, here is the quote again:

Focus, Work Smart, Execute Now, and Everything Else Will Follow.

Seriously, that is all you need to know.

So why wait?

The time to start becoming your best self is now.
It is only up to you.

Start focusing.

Then start working smart which leads to execution
(i.e. completing tasks).

Everything follows after that.

Even though those few words answer many questions,
it is not easy.

Striving to become your best self does take a lot of change,
self-motivation and even some sacrifice.

We feel we are so far away from that version of ourselves.
We feel that we can't get there.

Taking a quick step back, you have to define that "best self"
for yourself.

Your Best Self is the great individual you dream of being in all areas of your life, including your health, career and relationships.

It also includes reaching your potential, attaining goals and experiencing success that make you a happier and better human being who can reflect that positivity back to the world.

If you use the quote, the individual you dream of being will become your reality.

Reading too much on self-motivation (i.e. waiting to begin and not taking action) does not help us get there in the short or the long run.

It is much easier to read than take action. True.

It is easier to delay goals and not confront the challenge
of becoming our best self. True as well.

It is easier to accomplish what we want in the future,
rather than in the present. Very true.

As mentioned in Chapter 1, you only need these words to get you on that path:

Focus, Work Smart, Execute Now, and Everything Else Will Follow.

Think about each step (again) for a moment.

Take another moment.

Really think about how it fits together and where it fits with you.

Is it making more sense now?

Can you see how these words can positively impact your life?

If not, how do we start realizing that these are the only words you need?

It starts with looking at the quote as a process.

Each set of words feeds into the next one.

If you start and take each step, the process will be successful, but first <u>you</u> have to start.

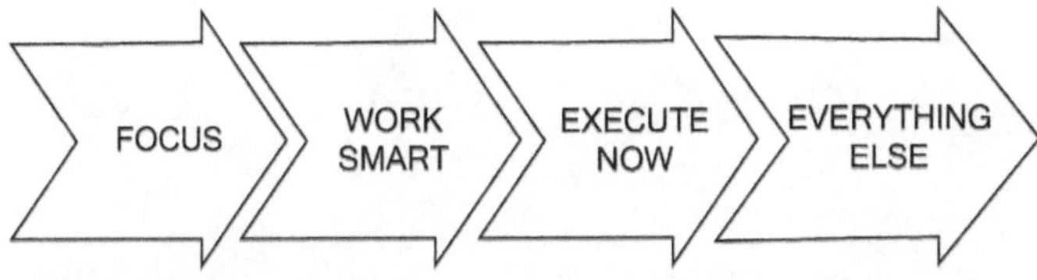

Doing so will get you on the path towards your best self.

That's it.

Seriously, you can stop reading now. And, to save you time, start applying those words to your life.

Good luck!

Was the quote not clear enough?

Were they not bold enough words to do so?

Still need to read more?

You don't need to read more.

Just implement this quote, which can be broken down into four digestible sections:

Focus

Work Smart

Execute Now

Everything Else Will Follow

25

Did that work? Are you still here?

Darn, it must not be because you are still reading.

Maybe it is more difficult than simply sharing some meaningful words.

Maybe this seemingly simple quote needs more explanation as to why it can be so significant in your life.

The reason why implementing it is difficult is because it takes effort and requires real, impactful change.

Perhaps we do need a little more detail to really illustrate the power of this quote.

After a more detailed analysis of the quote and explanation of its significance, you'll promise to put down this book and start?

Deal.

Chapter 4:
A Bit More Detail Before We Go

Breaking down each part of the quote answers the following questions:

- Why are those words so powerful?

- Why are they significant?

- Why do they work together?

Answering these questions will give you the necessary information to stop reading any further, but to do this, two definitions need to be introduced:

Motivation and Best Self.

Motivation

Primary definition of motivation: the general desire or willingness of someone to do something.

Real definition of motivation: an attitude which leads to the self-started actions we need to take to become our best selves.

Motivation is the driving factor for what enables us to focus, work smart and execute, so everything else can follow.

What motivates you?

Best Self

Your Best Self is the person you envisage yourself to be,
who reaches your personal and professional potential
day in and day out.

Attaining your best self is experienced through feelings of
fulfillment, positivity, happiness, accomplishment,
satisfaction and attainment.

Being your best self is confirmation that you have evolved
and taken ownership of your life.

What does your best self look like? Who do you want yourself
to be?

Think about those two definitions in your own life and now think about the quote.

Once you can answer those questions – knowing what motivates you and how you envision your best self – you can then see more clearly how the quote can have a positive impact, starting with focus.

Focus is the ability to concentrate on a single task or endeavor.
You <u>choose</u> to focus.

Once focused, you are in the mindset and position to work
smart.

To work smart means to put physical and mental effort towards
tasks and making progress on them.

Once you work smart, you will execute.

"Executing Now" means you have hit milestones, attained goals and completed tasks.

When you reach this part of the quote, you will start to feel satisfaction because you have seen things through.

Maybe even a bit of happiness.

Then what follows? Everything else.

If you can do those first three sections with purpose and success, happiness and results will follow in all areas of your life.

Little victories add up to big ones.

Results and progress towards your best self is inevitable when you follow the quote in that order.

Of course, there are many other quotes. But this one,
when executed, delivers both expected and bonus results.

Isn't it worth a try?

From here on in, right from this moment, it is up to you.

You are the source, the problem and the solution to your life.

It comes from within no matter what external factors we face.

What exactly is stopping you?

Of course, there are situations where you may not be ready.

Do you choose not to be ready, or are there serious impediments preventing you from being ready?

For example, an important requirement for being able to focus
is to put yourself in situations that give you the opportunity
for success.

If your situation is not conducive to your ability to focus,
immediate change is required.

To do so, simply avoid or remove yourself from situations that don't enable you to focus.

Figure out what your impediments are and work through them so you can.

That was a lot to throw at you.

So enough reading, waiting and thinking. The time to start doing is now.

You know what to do.

Go out and live these words.

It is up to you from this point.

Is that enough to get you to stop reading and start applying them to your life right now?

Yes, right now.

Not sometime in the future, but at this very moment.

You have that power (if **YOU** want to apply it).

That simple string of words is all you need.

Simple and effective.

To assist you, let's end this book again. You have the quote and the knowledge of what you want your best self to be, so now go and achieve it.

With this time so kindly given back, you can now get back to work.

That's it. You don't have to read anymore.

You can now take the time to do, _to take action_.

What a relief we don't have to wait any longer before we can become our best selves!

You may wish it was more complicated than that.

But there really isn't much more to it.

The rest of this book will be more of the same, but if it helps you to see this more clearly, perhaps read on.

Maybe you need a little more of a push.

And that really is all there is to say, so thank you for reading.

The End. Again.

Chapter 5:
Why Do We Feel We Need More Words?

Deceiving, isn't it?

We told you that you did not need to read further.

So why are you?

Even with further explanation, it is amazing how we still feel the need to overthink to try to find motivation and answers before acting.

When simple words are used, we feel we need to keep gathering more information before we can begin.

Regardless of external factors that we usually lean on as excuses for delay, we <u>choose</u> to prevent ourselves from starting this journey towards our best self.

External factors are not the only thing that holds us back.

Internal factors, our own inner mental battles, also stop us and are often the toughest to overcome.

The advantage of the quote is that those external factors and inner struggles can be disintegrated when we start applying it.

When you focus and work smart because you are in the zone of becoming your best self, there is no room for those external or internal negative forces to stop us.

There are many obstacles that we place in front of ourselves that do not exist in reality. They lead us to believe that it is easier to stay stagnant than start taking the steps to become our best self.

A whole book can be written on that.

Maybe it will be, but right now, the quickest way to reduce analysis (since you already *feel* and *know* what the obstacles are) is to lean on motivational words that get us through.

Know any?

Here is one you may already know, but reading it again may work:

Focus, Work Smart, Execute Now, and Everything Else
Will Follow.

Are those words starting to connect more?

Enough to put down this book and begin?

Guess there should have been a disclaimer to say that following this quote would not be easy.

Perhaps we need to take a step back (before we finally stop reading) to get a clearer understanding of how this quote can have an immediate positive impact on us.

Let's do that.

Chapter 6:
At the Nexus of Positive Change

This quote is so powerful as it stands, but when we take that big step back, the quote is positioned at the nexus of your current self and your best self as you live and experience life.

Do not underestimate the importance of focus as the first step. It allows you to create the environment where you can start becoming your best self, as this visual illustrates:

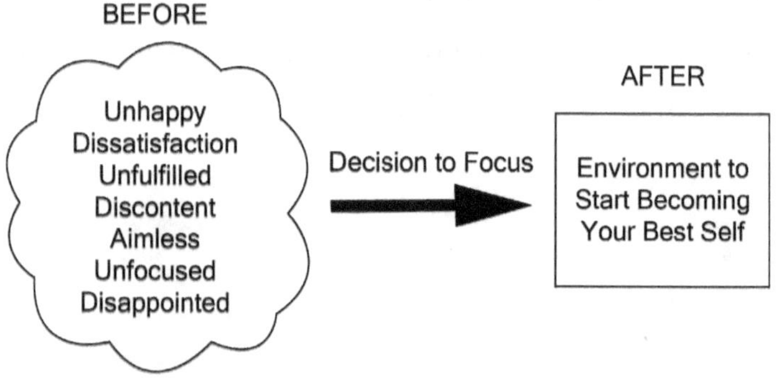

We need a turning point – a singular, critical moment when we make the switch from living as our current self to taking the first steps towards our best self.

Focus allows us to get to that point.

Whether it is a simple goal such as going for a walk each day or embarking on a new career path, the first necessary step which allows progress to be made is focus.

This quote can be applied anywhere on this planet – physical and virtual platforms – to everyone, in any situation, whether you are facing an obstacle or looking to build on your success from an already comfortable and thriving position.

It especially makes sense in today's distracting digital world where information moves at lightning speeds, continually creating distractions that prevent us from focusing.

(Although, it is important to state that the infinite access to information and tools can definitely assist when it can be positively utilized for your benefit.)

With thousands of other quotes that you can reference, each with their own meaning and application, this one can act at the center of everything you do, at the moment when you need it, no matter how big or small the task or goal is.

You are probably still thinking how difficult that is, right?

Well, it is difficult.

That difficulty in getting from where you are now to your best self is usually self-created.

Most of the obstacles we face in life are created in our imagination and put in front of us as if they exist in reality.

And that's why it is powerful.

The quote challenges you.

It tests you.

It forces you to look inwards and smacks you with the reality of your situation, which in most cases we back down from because it is easier to stay where we are and not seek something more amazing for our lives.

When you get that feeling of defeat at those moments (before even beginning), guess what the best words are to reference and realign yourself on the "best self" path?

Focus, Work Smart, Execute Now, and Everything Else
Will Follow.

Take a moment to assess your progress, then with that said...

. . . enough thinking.

You already have enough to begin.

So now, another attempt will be made to save you the time so you can get back to becoming your best self without more of these pesky words in the way.

One final step, and then we are done.

Go back and read Chapter 1 for one last time, and then start enjoying this exciting new journey you are about to embark on to get to your best self.

After processing those words again, having the only words you need, you ended up back here.

Don't worry, this is normal.

When we read any kind of motivational words, we tend to say to ourselves, "That makes sense and I agree with it, and I'll put it into action, but just not yet."

Why do we think that?

The short answer is, we don't know what to focus on, or are overwhelmed because there are too many things to focus on.

Or maybe we are not ready.

Let's work that out.

Firstly, if you know what to focus on in your life, to give you your time back, feel free to go to the Final Message so you can finish this book (and get back to doing what you know you need to do).

If you don't know what to focus on, read further, but when you do know, promise that you will (finally) put this book down.

Chapter 7:
Knowing What to Focus On

"Focus" is difficult, which is why it is the first word in the quote.

The challenge we may face at every moment is that we don't know what to do or how to begin.

Focus:

It means to stop avoiding what you are meant to do.

It means not making any excuses for ourselves.

It means taking ownership and initiative.

It means taking accountability of our actions.

To "focus", we need to know what step comes before "focus".

To help overcome the hazy cloud of our current self, here are a few examples to get you thinking about the types of things which you may need to change about your life so that you can focus:

- Making some short-term and long-term goals.

- Removing yourself from negative situations or getting away from negative people.

- Getting out of bad relationships and partnerships.

- Registering for schooling, upskilling, training or certifications.

- Saving some money (i.e. sacrificing wasteful spending) and investing in yourself.

- Changing bad habits that are affecting your mental clarity and physical health.

- Changing a job or career which you know isn't your calling.

- Saying no to social engagements that suck your energy and waste your time.

It's not that complicated when we zero in on what is preventing us from becoming our best self, and realize the tricks our minds are playing on us.

There is a lot to align, change and resolve before focusing, but beginning (and not dwelling on obstacles) is the way to allow yourself to focus.

Some questions to guide you:

- What are my goals?

- What do I want to focus on?

- What am I trying to achieve?

- What are the first steps I need to take?

- What are the second and third steps I need to take?

- What is the 20th step of that process and steps further down the line?

Just imagine them. No need for the answers to be perfect. That will come.

For now, having so many questions and answers across many areas of our life accumulating in our minds simultaneously can feel overwhelming when you think about them all at once.

Right now, isolate the top goals – the ones you really want to see manifested in your life as soon as possible.

Then pick one thing you can do that will get you on the path towards that goal and your best self.

There is no need to add pressure on yourself to finish perfectly on day one. You'll get there eventually if you focus on something achievable now and start taking small steps each day.

The approach for this step is not intended to cover all aspects of motivation, only that singular moment when you know you should (must?) do what you know you need to do.

There should be some urgency though on picking something as opposed to indifference and not focusing on anything.

Overthinking is our enemy.

Doing is our ally.

What if, right now, you were to pick one thing and make that your focus? Then you will be ready to go.

Is there something you really want to focus on?

Do you know what that one thing would be?

Think about that for a few seconds.

Just one thing. One task.

To help you, complete this sentence by filling it in with a personal goal or task of any type:

Right now, I will focus on _______________________________________.

Examples:

- *Right now, I will focus on getting healthier.*

- *Right now, I will focus on that school project I need to get done.*

- *Right now, I will focus on finding myself a better career, one that I have always wanted to do.*

- *Right now, I want to address a bad habit that I have.*

- *Right now, I will stop wasting time with people that do not encourage me to be my best self.*

The reason that focus starts the quote is that it assists you at the moment when you transform not doing into doing.

Right at that nexus is where focus matters most.

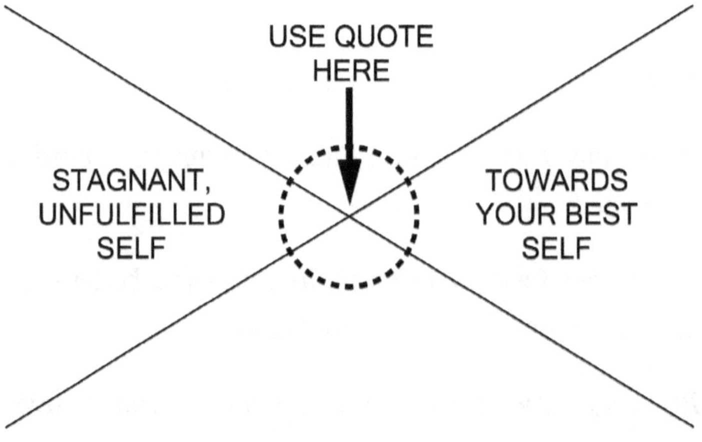

To get to that transformative point, understand that focus is a decision, not just a thought.

Focus begins your journey from your unfulfilled self towards your best.

Focus requires action, and also leads you to action.

Filled in the blank?

Good.

You know what to focus on, so stop reading and start working smart on that and only that.

Manifest the quote from here on in.

So why are you reading further when you already know what to focus on?

You know that one thing you can start with. Go do it!

Enough thinking.

Enough analyzing.

Enough reading.

Enough waiting.

Time to do. Time to work smart.

Chapter 8: Working Smarter

If you have a goal and are focused on it, you give yourself the ability to work smart.

Working smart is different from working hard.

Working smart is all about saving time spent thinking, and focusing on time doing instead. It is also known as taking action with purpose.

Your time becomes dedicated to a goal, initiated by your focus on the direction of that goal.

Working hard does not guarantee that you will make progress towards your goal.

Working smart means understanding the simplest tasks that will help get you there, and implementing them.

Ask yourself:

- What are these tasks?

- What actions do I need to take now to work smart?

- What steps will lead to progress towards my goal?

- What can I do right now?

Perform this simple, self-reflective and motivational exercise to figure this out:

I need to take these actions to make progress towards the goal I am focused on:

1. ____

2. ____

3. ____

4. ____

5. ____

When you have those filled in, now ask when you are going to do this?

It's a trick question.

The answer is:

Now.

Now is the moment to take action and work smart to complete those tasks.

Yes, now!

If not now because of some excuse taking over your mind, put those obstacles and challenges to the side, and start.

No matter what, it is up to you to take action, even just for a few minutes to start.

You can wait for the future. That's up to you. We always postpone things to the future because it gives us a pass in the present.

It is always easier that way, which is why it is a path that many follow.

Procrastination. Being a dilettante. That's an easy way to live life, but remaining stagnant is definitely not as fulfilling.

That's what you may have been doing up to this point.
And how has that worked out for you?

You need to realize that you don't have to wait.
You are focused and ready to work.

You are free to start now, but saying "I plan to work smart"
can only take you so far.

The action of working smart is required.

Now you see why working smart matters and why it is different to just working hard or simply being indifferent.

Time to do things differently than before.

Since you have come this far, you now know all you need to know. With that said, feel free to stop reading at this moment and start working smart.

Isn't it a relief that you can now take action and not think so much? Aren't you relieved that you have the answers to your questions and don't have to wonder what you should be doing?

Perfect. Now go!

Well, guess that reminder didn't work?

When you take these actions, perhaps you may question whether you are working smart versus working aimlessly?

That's easy to gauge.

You usually only know if you have worked smart after it happens and you see the results.

You will look back on the day or week afterwards and see that you did.

If you are having difficulty focusing or figuring out what to focus on, use the ABC Method found in *40 Is the New 80: A Semi-Practical Guide to the Halftime of Life*.

Here is a summary of the exercise:

Every day make a list, mental or written, on the top three goals you need to focus on that day. These can be as big or small as you want them to be.

Then think about the first few tasks for that specific action item.

Break it down as simply as possible.

Here are examples that relate to career, physical/mental health and finance.

Today I need to:

A. Perform job searching for my new dream role.

B. Go for a long walk and do 5 minutes of meditation.

C. Save money by cooking my own meal.

What are your ABC tasks for today?

A. ____

B. ____

C. ____

This ABC process enables you to identify exactly what you need to do at each moment on each given day.

Working smart is getting those singular tasks done that contribute towards each goal you have set for yourself.

By completing those tasks in an efficient way as close to "the now" allows you, you have worked smart because you dedicated your time to doing what you set out to focus on.

You can look back on the day, week, month or year and see that you have made progress.

And progress is an aggregate of all those individual tasks that you listed and the new ones that you added on.

Whoa, just thinking about how far we have come.

We have read over 100 pages.

How about we end this analysis and give you some of your time back to get those ABC tasks done?

Are you beginning to see how time is becoming more valuable?

Why waste it?

Time progresses at a consistent pace, and the amount of time you have left counts down each day, so make the time count for something.

Will it keep being wasted or will it be productively utilized?

Oh, you're too busy at the moment?

No time right now?

Then when?

To understand time in the context of your life, you need to estimate how much time you have left on this planet.

The following table will help you to understand the value of time and how it counts down based on your age and the average lifespan.

<u>Time Remaining at Each Age Until 80 Years Of Age*</u>

	30yo	40yo	50yo	60yo	70yo
Hours	438,000	350,400	262,800	175,200	87,600
Days	18,250	14,600	10,950	7,300	3,650
Weeks	2,600	2,080	1,560	1,040	520
Months	600	480	360	240	120

estimated time based on global average human mortality of 80 years old

Time ticks away whether you like it or not.

The time left in the above table is based on living to 80 years of age (a truly marvelous human feat!). However, not all are gifted this much time and some are gifted more.

We may feel there is lots of time left, but when you actually think about the amount of time, it shows how little we have left to start working smart towards our best self.

(This should prompt you to read the quote one more time as a last bit of motivation, then be on your way.)

As an advantage, no matter what, at this moment, you have 100% of your life left.

Now, this very moment of your life, is your time to do what you wish.

Time to focus.

Time to work smart.

When you finish those first steps and truly understand that point, then you should read on.

[Strategically placed blank page to see if you stopped reading]

Midpoint Message

Wait. That was a little too quick.

Did that work? Did you stop reading?

Did you go and *do*? Did you focus and work smart?

We are halfway through analyzing the quote.

Isn't it exciting when we start to focus on ourselves for once in life.

Feel good already?

Depending on what age you read this at, you will either feel awakened to what you can be or reawakened to what you want to be.

Those are tough steps because they require a change of behavior, a change of attitude and a change of habit.

You made it halfway, even though that wasn't the intention of this book. Time could have been spent working towards your best self. Do you have enough insight now to take action and make progress? Is it enough now to put the book down, focus and work smart?

Manifesting the quote requires dedication and action, which is even more challenging, but an advantage is that the smarter you work, the luckier you get.

The more stuff starts to happen *for you* (not only *to you*).

If you are reading this book up to this point, you are more ready than you know.

It shows you care and are invested, and that you truly want to become your best self.

You must use that truth.

Since we've only analyzed half of the quote, ask: Is that enough or do we need to cover the other half?

What is the result of successfully implementing the first two parts of the quote?

If you focus and work smart you will undoubtedly...

. . . Execute.

Chapter 9:
Executing to Completion

If you focus and work smart, you will see results today.

That is to say, you successfully executed.

To execute is to complete those ABC tasks.

Most importantly, it is seeing these things through, not stopping halfway, or even worse, not even starting.

Executing is the result of putting in the smart work to allow yourself to hit milestones and attain goals.

When you start executing now, you will find that you feel great because you set out to do something and you did it. You will want more of this feeling, which will propel you further towards your best self.

That is why executing feels amazing.

We have stepped onto our own path and realized that we can in fact do the things we dreamt of doing.

Those big moments of success, accomplishment and achievement are an aggregate of all the tasks completed when you execute.

Seeing tasks through and getting to the execution stage seems challenging.

Perhaps it *is* necessary to read on from here and not stop reading just yet.

Being so far into a motivational book that only requires one page to be read, shows how difficult it is to materialize these types of quotes.

When we read them, we easily understand them and even agree most of the time, but when it comes to putting them into action, we freeze up more often than not.

Perhaps we are afraid of success?

Perhaps we are apprehensive of the changes we will have to make in our lives?

Perhaps we are fearful of becoming our best selves?

Execution resolves all these questions if we allow it.

When you successfully execute, this new feeling may feel unfamiliar, because you stopped being your unfulfilled self and became one with purpose.

This transformation is not about being perfectly stoic at every moment, but it should be a high percentage.

What percentage of your time is dedicated to these pursuits?

40%? 80%?

How much time in your life will you dedicate to executing?

The more time you dedicate, the more you start to see a path forward.

You see purpose.

This propels you more as you further realize your goals are within reach.

You can complicate it all you like, but the simplicity of realizing you have a unique purpose (across all humans across all history!) inevitably leads to huge increases in growth.

Executing also motivates you to continue.

It motivates you to start the process once again, but with the addition of a new dimension.

The quote actually works cyclically, not just linearly.

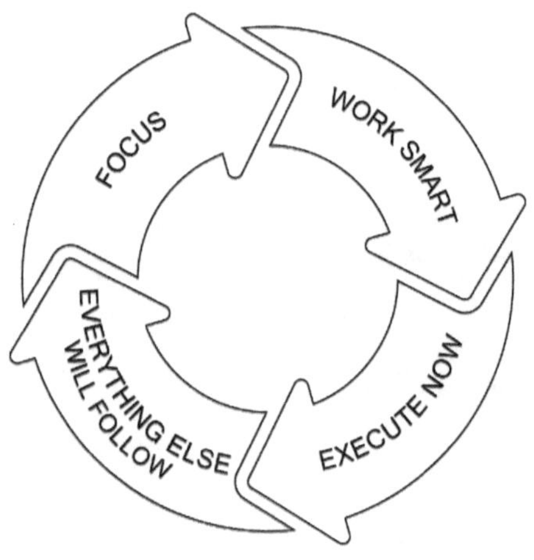

The more you execute, the more tasks you finish and milestones you will hit, which feeds into self-motivation required to keep on doing.

This is where your focused energy and dedication through smart work and execution begins to line up more opportunities.

In other words, Everything Else Will Follow from there.

Before we proceed, was that enough to motivate you so you could stop reading, or are you still here?

Do you need a bit more of a push?

Perhaps a little more insight into this final part of the quote will get you on the path you are meant to be on. The one you envision your life to be.

We can go that route, but after this, you'll promise to begin living your elevated life?

So be it.

Chapter 10:
Everything Else Will (Inevitably) Follow

This is the best part of the quote because it states that things will start to happen in your life when you focus, work smart and execute now.

Overcoming obstacles, especially getting out of your own way, allows life to open up, potential to be reached and opportunities to be revealed.

Getting to this stage reaffirms you are on the right path and moving closer towards your best self.

What is that "everything else" part all about?

Both personally and professionally, when you set out to do what you are meant to do and start hitting goals, you inevitably:

Get <u>results</u>.

Make <u>progress</u>.

Experience <u>accomplishment</u>.

Followed by a rush of super good feelings, including:

Satisfaction.

Excitement.

Proudness.

Success.

Happiness.

Confidence.

Maybe even a genuine smile.

You will know for sure when waking up ready to seize the day, not dreading it. And at the end of the day, feeling like it was the best one yet.

These feelings are the manifestation of that simple string of words.

Why is this so?

All these results have the opportunity to follow because you are in the right mindset to succeed. You are also peeling back the layers of your best self that were in you all along.

If you follow the quote, you'll notice a better attitude, and you'll gravitate towards more positive and supportive people. You will navigate out of bad situations and be in better mental and physical health (due to less stress).

Your focus, smart work ethic and execution got you here.

Feel good about that.

You'll start to see that you *can* do it and realize how powerful
you actually are (which you really knew all this time even
before reading the first chapter, but have now reaffirmed
to yourself!).

Throughout the process, however, you will not experience perfect progress or results every day.

Some results may be of failure and near misses, but you will be able to continue forward because you can use those as lessons to learn and grow. Through those challenges, you will be taking steps towards your best self without even realizing.

Becoming aware of this and understanding that failures are part of the journey, will demonstrate you are working towards your best self.

With this self-created force behind you, you empower yourself
to keep going and rise higher.

You'll be in a better position to focus and be more motivated
to work smarter.

You'll be more satisfied with your position at any point as you
will be experiencing a real transformation.

This new growth continues to feed into your motivation to
focus, work smart and...

...well, you get it.

When you have applied the quote a few times and begin to see progress, you will rise upwards, elevating you to your best self!

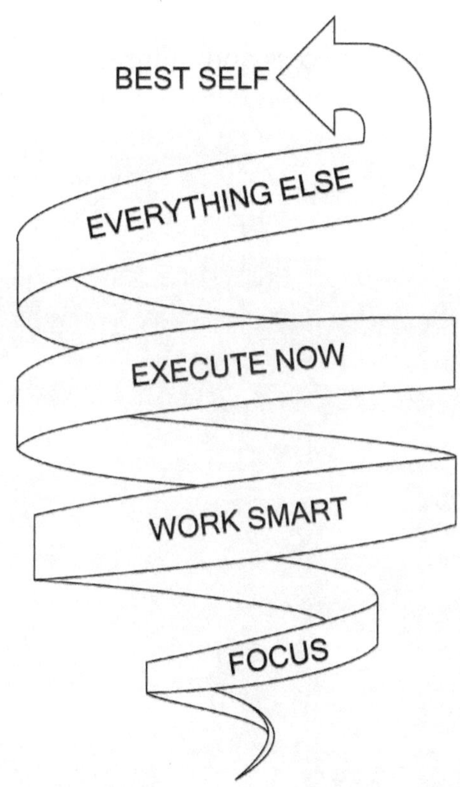

With your dedicated efforts, you will turn this quote from just words into a habit, a prompt, and a way of life that will always lead to great things.

Your efforts and dedication allow those wins to happen.

It all starts with you – success and failure.

Doing so, you will start to see the emergence of the best version of yourself.

"Everything else", all those things you dream of and maybe never thought you would do, will happen in your life.

Now that you have read all you know you need to, are you ready to implement these words?

Do you want to do this?

Do you actually want to implement these words in your life?

Good.

Then go and...

Focus, Work Smart, Execute Now, and Everything Else
Will Follow.

Thought that meant now?

Yes, like right now!

Don't overthink.

Don't stop yourself. Don't make yourself your worst enemy.

<u>You</u> have <u>you</u>, the most powerful force and asset in your life.

Surprising and seemingly too easy, those words are all you need.

Remember:

Focus starts the process.

Smart work habits make progress.

Execution (i.e. seeing things through) allows your goals
to materialize.

If you do the first three things in succession, results will happen,
and everything will follow.

Over time, these simple words will become a part of your life where the steps and borders dissolve; it will no longer be only linear, cyclical and spiral, but all of the words will work simultaneously in different intensities towards different goals.

To summarize, again, you only need to remember those simple words to propel you towards your best self.

You know what you need to do.

So right now. . .

. . . and GO and DO.

Chapter 11:
Overcoming the Fear of Success

It was worth the attempt.

It is amazing how much effort it takes to stop reading and start focusing.

Starting is difficult. To sit down and reevaluate. To stop aimlessly doing distracting and fruitless activities, it takes self-discipline.

If you are reading this part, then you may still feel that you are not ready.

Isolate very quickly why you have not begun. We all have different reasons, but let's just look at you for a moment.

Are you fearful of change?

Are you afraid to leave your comfort zone and start doing things you've never done before?

Are you scared of becoming your best self?

Are you standing in your own way and stopping it happening?

To ease these mental blocks and obstacles, remember these three ways of thinking which can help you to overcome them:

Progress over Perfection.

Momentum over Stagnation.

Flight over Fight.

The key theme is action. Specifically, taking action on a path towards your best self.

No need to wait for perfection.

Remember, your *best self* does not have to be your *perfect self*.

Your time on this earth is incredibly valuable and finite (remember, time is ticking away!), and we've wasted enough time reading.

So just a few more pages, okay?

Reading more would just distract you. Isn't that right?

There is time for reading, but there must be more time for action.

Since you invested into this book, you may as well have a few more pages of quotes we all love to read, even though the quote covers what you need.

You don't have to read them, but here they are…

Ha!

You don't need any more words!

You don't need anything else. You know that by now!

Just follow the quote to become your best self.

Adding more quotes, even though they may be useful, would just be another excuse to keep on reading, and waiting to become ready even though you already are.

Yes, it is that simple.

So why do we complicate everything?

We complicate everything because it is easier.

It is easier to watch from the bleachers with an unfulfilled lookout on life instead of getting in the boxing ring with yourself.

(Sometimes analogies work to get the fire started within us.)

Is there something standing in your way?

Are there obstacles?

Could it be friends or family that are blocking you?

Could there be societal roadblocks that you believe are in front
of you (but that you know within you that you have the power
to overcome?).

Do you let those obstacles rule your life?

If you answered 'yes' to any of those questions, overcome them by taking yourself out of that situation and doing the work.

Start with focusing on something. List your ABC tasks.

You have the choice to make positive change if you want it.

Final Message:
Why Do You Only Need These Words?

Only a few words were required to create a powerful quote that you will (hopefully) use right now to become your best self.

Take those words and materialize them. They will fit so perfectly into your life if you want them to and if you choose to apply them. The quote can be repeated over and over, but if they remain just hopeful words, they will have no value in your life.

More words do not make motivation better. *You* make yourself better. The advantage you have is the quote works in any situation, regardless of your obstacles.

Whether you can control it or not, still focus.

Whether it takes more effort than you thought at first, still work smart.

Whether the results are what you expected or not, still execute.

No matter what, still go through the process, then everything else will follow.

Simply visualizing, dreaming and believing does not work in practice. The action of doing is what propels you forward towards your best self.

This best self is not your perfect self. It is more an enhanced version of yourself who is finally fulfilling your purpose. You define what that is in your current situation. Although our definition of our best self changes, sometimes often, that is what you need to aspire to each day.

You'll know you are there when you look back on life and see the point where you decided to make a change, and the benefits that resulted from making that decision to focus and work smarter.

Now is the time to wrap this up and give you no excuses not to focus, work smart and execute, so everything such as success, happiness, accomplishment can follow.

We've already used so many pages to explain something so simple. So from here onwards, it should not be <u>as difficult</u> for us to stop reading and just get to it.

Time to do it. Time to do it now.

Perhaps you are still questioning yourself. That you can't do it or that success is impossible. When in doubt, use the quote at that critical and opportune moment when you know you could be fulfilling your purpose.

Start with just one task. One simple thing to focus on. It is only you who can initiate it.

Let's give you your time back right now to do so.

You have the words you need.

Acknowledgments

Only to the muses that work through us.

About the Author

P.J. Staz is a human being.
He currently resides on
planet Earth.

Other Titles by P.J. Staz

*40 is the New 80: A Semi-Practical
Guide to the Halftime of Life*

♦

*Failure Starts with You: Unmotivational Quotes to Guide
You Nowhere*

♦

*Where is the Universe?: A Short Journey to the Furthest Points
in Outer Space*

♦

*Where Are Those Satellites Going?:
A Quick Orbital Adventure of
Earth's Selfie Takers*